Mammals are thos[e] *entirely, or in part, o[f]* *having mammary glan[ds]* [used] *their young. Mammal[s]* *temperature remaining* [constant regardless of] *variations in outside temperature. There are three main groups of living mammals, and each group is represented in Australia as follows:*

(1) *The* Monotremes, *or egg-laying mammals, by the Platypus and Echidna (Spiny Ant-eater). These are found nowhere else in the world outside the Australian region. Of all the mammals, the* Monotremes *are most closely related to their reptilian ancestors. Besides laying large-yolked eggs, they have retained the reptilian cloaca or single-opening ('mono-treme') which receives the ends of the intestine and the urinary and genital ducts. However,* Monotremes *also exhibit highly specialised characteristics such as loss of teeth.*

(2) *The* Marsupials, *or pouched mammals, by the* Kangaroos, Possums, Wombats, Bandicoots *and* Dasyurids. *This group also is largely confined to the Australian region with some species living in the Americas. The young are born in a very immature condition but are able to crawl into the pouch (or* marsupium) *where they attach themselves to a teat. In the pouch, the young are protected and carried during their early life.*

(3) *The* Placentals, *or 'higher' mammals, by Rats and Mice, Bats, Seals and Whales. The young are attached inside the mother's body to the* placenta, *a structure richly supplied with blood vessels to nourish the developing embryo. Thus the young can grow to a more highly developed stage before birth.* Placentals *are not as numerous in Australia as they are in most other countries.*

A Ladybird Book
Series 691

'*Australian Mammals*' *is the second in a series of Ladybird books about animals of the world. In each book, superb, full-coloured illustrations are supported by an informative text.*

This book describes the fascinating mammal population of Australia - those most primitive of mammals which survived, and remained as they were, when the land bridge to the rest of the world was severed by the sea. Mammals of New Zealand are also included.

A coloured chart shows the various types of habitat of the Australian mammals. An index is given and also - at the back - the various Orders and Families to which the animals belong.

The publishers wish to acknowledge the assistance of Miss Patricia M. McDonald of The Australian Museum, Sydney, when preparing the revised edition of this book.

AUSTRALIAN MAMMALS

written and illustrated by
JOHN LEIGH-PEMBERTON

Publishers: Ladybird Books Ltd . Loughborough
© Ladybird Books Ltd (formerly Wills & Hepworth Ltd) 1970, 1972
Printed in England

Echidna (or Spiny Ant-eater)

Length, head and body 35–50 cm.

Spiny ant-eaters live mainly in open scrubby or rocky country. They feed on 'white ants' or termites and other insects which they collect on their long sticky, tongues after tearing open the nests with the powerful claws on their front feet. They have no teeth, food being crushed between hard ridges on the palate and base of the tongue.

The body of the spiny ant-eater is covered with fur interspersed on the back with sharp spines; for protection the animal buries itself with only the spines protruding, or rolls up into a spiky ball.

At breeding time the females develop a pouch-like fold of skin on the abdomen into which the single (rarely more) leathery-shelled egg is laid. Here it is incubated for about ten days, the mother curling her body round it. On hatching, the young, only 12 mm. in length, is fed with milk from the mother, not from teats but from special pores in her skin. The young remains in the temporary pouch for about seven weeks by which time it has developed spines. It is then hidden under cover by the mother.

Male Spiny Ant-eaters have spurs on their ankles, connected to glands which are mildly poisonous. Spiny Ant-eaters are found throughout Australia and Tasmania in suitable country, and a larger species lives in New Guinea and nearby islands.

4

0 7214 0258 5

Platypus

Length, head and body   *40 cm.*
Length of tail   *12 cm.*

In addition to other Monotreme features, the Platypus possesses webbed feet and a soft, sensitive snout, shaped like a duck's bill but unlike it in other respects.

Platypuses live near rivers and lakes along the eastern coastlands of Australia and in Tasmania. They feed on crayfish, worms and small fish, hunting them on the bottom of streams and lakes. They can stay submerged for up to five minutes, during which time the eyes and ears are closed by a fold of skin, direction and location of prey being ascertained by nerve-endings in the sensitive snout. In the bank a shallow tunnel is made, sometimes with several openings and often among the roots of a tree close to the water level.

In the breeding season, the female Platypus digs a special nesting burrow, which may be up to 20 feet long, with a nesting chamber at the end, lined with grass and leaves. One to three (usually two) leathery-shelled eggs, 18 mm. long and with very large yolks, are laid. The female Platypus does not develop a pouch and never leaves her eggs, which she incubates by curling her body round them until they hatch in about ten days. The young are then fed with milk through pores in the mother's skin.

Like the Spiny Ant-eater, the adult male Platypus carries spurs on its ankles. These are more poisonous than those of the Spiny Ant-eater and are capable of causing great pain—and even partial paralysis in any attacker.

Once hunted for its fur and in danger of becoming extinct, the platypus is now protected by law and is increasing in numbers.

Crested-tailed Marsupial 'Rat' (*above*)

Length, head and body	17 cm.
Length of tail	13·5 cm.

Jerboa Marsupial 'Mouse' (*below*)

Length, head and body	10 cm.
Length of tail	12 cm.

One of the principal marsupial families is that of *Dasyuridae*, to which both these species belong. Although many members of this family are referred to as 'rats' and 'mice', and even as 'cats', they are in fact in no way related to these animals. The names given to them by early explorers are misleading, although in appearance there is a resemblance to those mammals after which they have been named.

This resemblance is due to what is known as the effect of 'convergence'—the tendency of animals living the same sort of life in similar conditions to develop identical physical features.

The Crested-tailed Marsupial 'Rat' is a carnivorous and insectivorous inhabitant of semi-desert country. It is seen very little, as it is rare as well as being nocturnal. It is believed to produce up to six young at a birth which, when born, measure no more than four millimetres in length; this is about the length of the word 'the', as printed in this book.

Another inhabitant of scrub and desert is the Jerboa Marsupial 'Mouse', in appearance remarkably like some rodent species such as the Jerboas of Africa and Asia. These little creatures are nocturnal, insectivorous and, in spite of their minute size, aggressive. They spend the day in burrows.

Six young are born at a birth, and crawl into the pouch which, as with most other dasyurids, opens to the rear. There are two species—both in danger of extinction.

Mulgara (Crested-tailed Marsupial Mouse)

| Length, head and body | 18 cm. |
| Length of tail | 10 cm. |

The Mulgara, a member of the family *Dasyuridae*, lives in the sandy deserts of central Australia. Although it looks like a small rodent, it is in fact principally flesh-eating and hunts its prey, which consists of insects, small reptiles and rodents, with the stealth and ferocity of a typical carnivore.

Like other members of its family, it has a great many needle-sharp teeth and is able to open its mouth unusually wide. During plagues of House Mice in its area, the Mulgara quickly hunts them down and destroys them. The prey is most methodically eaten, the skin being turned neatly inside out from head to tail.

This animal is chiefly nocturnal, but also spends some time sunning itself outside its breeding burrow—as do many small members of this family. Seven young are born at a birth and attach themselves unaided to nipples in the mother's pouch, which is nothing more than a fold of skin. Here they remain for about a month. The time during which the young develop inside the mother's body before they are born—called the gestation period—is about thirty days; this is rather longer than for most small marsupials.

As desert dwellers they can survive for long periods without drinking, or even eating succulent plants. It seems they can get enough water from their ordinary diet. They are also able to withstand extremes of heat and cold.

Tuan (Brush-tailed Phascogale) (*above*)	Length, head and body	20 cm.
	Length of tail	19 cm.
Sminthopsis (Fat-tailed Marsupial Mouse) (*below*)	Length, head and body	8 cm.
	Length of tail	6 cm.

Most of the mouse-like members of the *Dasyuridae* family are silent, but the Tuan makes a series of sounds, from a cough to a bird-like 'chit-chit'; it also claps with its hands and 'drums' with its tail. Two species of Tuan are between them found throughout much of Australia, but not in Tasmania.

This nocturnal animal inhabits wooded country and lives in the trees, where it builds nests of leaves and twigs; it is in many ways rather like a squirrel.

Tuans are carnivorous and include birds in their diet, as well as lizards and insects. Two young are born at a birth and are fully mature at seven months old, although they spend the first nine weeks in the mother's pouch.

The little Sminthopsis looks remarkably like the shrews and Elephant Shrews of the rest of the world. However, as a *Dasyurid* it is truly carnivorous and insectivorous. It is found in Australia, Tasmania and New Guinea in a variety of habitats from humid forests to sandy desert. There are about ten species.

Although so small, it will kill and eat mice and lizards as well as insects, and some species store food in the fatty base of the tail. Moths are sometimes caught by jumping at them from the ground.

The average number of young is six, and these are kept in a well-developed, backward-facing pouch by the mother. When only half-grown the young are able to catch insects for themselves.

Tiger Cat

Length, head of body   70 cm.
Length of tail   50 cm.

Of the carnivorous marsupials of the mainland of Australia, the Tiger Cat is the largest. It is found in eastern and south-eastern Australia and Tasmania in the dense woodlands of forest country. It is not a 'cat' at all, of course, but a member of the family *Dasyuridae* and related to the little mouse-like creatures of that family.

This extremely active and tough animal is mainly nocturnal and spends much of its time on the ground; but it will also climb trees and appears in daylight if the sun is not too bright. The Tiger Cat will hunt quite large animals such as wallabies, and it will raid poultry farms, killing quite indiscriminately. It can be distinguished from the other Australian and New Guinea Native Cats, of which there are five species altogether, not only by its greater size but also by the spotted tail.

The gestation period is a mere twenty-one days, at the end of which about six young—no more than seven millimetres long—are born. They are kept in a backward-facing pouch, where they attach themselves for seven weeks to the mother's nipples. At this age their eyes begin to open, and they become independent at eighteen weeks.

Tiger Cats scream and hiss when angry, but this is said to be nothing more than bluff, and it is unlikely that they would attack a human being. They are not as plentiful as they once were, except in Tasmania. For some undiscovered reason, males are more common than females.

Quoll (Eastern Native Cat)

Length, head and body 40 cm.
Length of tail 25 cm.

The so-called 'Native Cats' of Australia and Tasmania resemble to a great extent the martens and mongooses among placental mammals. They are carnivorous, eating small animals up to the size of a rabbit, and their diet also includes fish and insects. Although mainly nocturnal, they sometimes sun themselves during the day, and all of them are agile climbers, particularly when hunting birds.

The Quoll, or Eastern Native Cat, is now found only in a few places in south-eastern Australia and in Tasmania. It was formerly much more widely spread but, like many Australian mammals, it is becoming more scarce. Small colonies survived in isolated pockets in the suburbs of cities such as Sydney and Hobart, but even these are now disappearing. Its normal habitat is in forest or open woodland.

This Native Cat is usually olive-brown spotted with white but there is also a less common black or grey variety, litters of mixed colours being quite usual. Females have eight nipples, but often produce more than twenty young at a time, so that only those which attach themselves to a teat in the pouch can survive.

These animals live among rocks or in hollow logs in which they sometimes make a rough nest of dry vegetation.

The other Native Cats are the Western Native Cat of south-western and central Australia, the Northern Native Cat of the coastal districts of Queensland and the northern territories, and its close relative, the New Guinean Native Cat. All these are members of the family *Dasyuridae*, but are placed in separate species.

Because of persecution, introduced predators and disease, all of them are, regrettably, becoming rare.

Tasmanian Devil

Found in modern times only in Tasmania, the Tasmanian 'Devil' was, until the introduction of the Dingo (p. 48), found also on the Australian mainland. This tough, rather bear-like marsupial inhabits dense undergrowth or rocky caves, where it builds nests of leaves and grass. It is a member of the extraordinarily varied *Dasyuridae* family, and like them is carnivorous and nocturnal.

As regards its way of life and its structure, it is the marsupial equivalent of the Hyaena, for it is a scavenger equipped with incredibly powerful jaws and massive teeth. Like other *Dasyuridae*, the opening of its jaws—called the 'gape'—is very wide.

This powerful animal is one of the few in the world which consumes the whole of its prey—bones, skin, fur or feathers; nothing is left. Anything up to the size of a sheep, providing it is sick or dying, and including poisonous snakes, is killed and eaten.

Three or four young are born in each litter and are kept in a totally enclosed pouch—an unusual feature which is only developed at breeding time and is peculiar to this mammal.

As with other marsupials, the young when born are in a very immature state—blind, deaf and hairless. Only twelve millimetres long at birth, they nevertheless have lungs which work, a nervous system, a beating heart and fairly well developed front legs equipped with claws, which enable them to climb unaided into the mother's pouch. Here they draw milk from the mother's teats and remain in the pouch for fifteen weeks.

Thylacine
(Tasmanian 'Wolf' Tasmanian 'Tiger')

Length, head and body   120 cm.
Length of tail   60 cm.

This remarkable animal once inhabited the mainland of Australia and, in the distant past, New Guinea as well. It is now confined to the mountainous western part of Tasmania, and during the last fifty years has declined so greatly in numbers that at times it has been presumed to be extinct. However, every now and then traces of its presence—some fur in a trap, the remains of a nest or even an actual sighting —indicate that it still exists, but it is just about the rarest mammal in the world.

Exterminated on the Australian mainland by the Dingo, the Thylacine (the word means 'pouched dog with wolf head'), is the largest marsupial carnivore. It is nocturnal, and will kill almost any other animal. Early sheep farmers in Tasmania paid large bounties for dead Thylacines, and by 1914 they had almost vanished.

Thylacines are extraordinarily dog-like, even whining, barking and growling. They have dog-like feet and teeth, but their hindquarters are more powerfully built with the thickened base of the tail giving more of a resemblance to the Kangaroos.

Forty years ago these animals could be seen in zoos. The last one in captivity died in Hobart Zoo in 1933, and the last one in the London Zoo in 1931.

The pouch, as with members of the family *Dasyuridae*, opens backwards, and there are four young in each litter. For its size the Thylacine has the widest 'gape' (mouth opening) of any mammal.

20

Numbat (Banded 'Ant-eater')

Length, head and body   24 cm.
Length of tail   17 cm.

In a family (*Myrmecobiidae*) by itself, the Numbat is a somewhat unusual Australian marsupial in that it does not possess a pouch. The young of this charming, squirrel-like animal attach themselves to the mother's nipples which, as with other marsupials, expand in their mouths, thus anchoring them securely. There are usually four young at a birth which, when half-grown, have round, puppy-like faces, and only later develop the long, thin snout of the adult.

Numbats are found mostly in south-western Australia, although a much rarer red form is found in central Australia as well. They are insect-eaters, their principal articles of diet being termites or ants; these are collected on a very long, cylindrical tongue. Oddly enough, in view of this diet, the Numbat has more teeth (50) than any other marsupial, although when caught it never attempts to bite. It also has a bony palate like that of other termite eaters.

Very strong claws and forelegs enable the Numbat to excavate hollow logs, not only in search of insects, but also in order to make itself a shelter. This is occupied at night for, unlike most small mammals, the Numbat is diurnal. It spends a great deal of time lying in the sun or scampering about among the eucalyptus logs which cover the floor of its woodland habitat.

Brush fires, forest clearance and introduced predators, such as dogs, are reducing the Numbat's numbers, and although not at present threatened with extinction, they need protection as do so many of the Australian mammals.

Banana Rat (*above*)	Length, head and body	15 cm.
	Length of tail	14 cm.
Short-nosed Bandicoot (*below*)	Length, head and body	35 cm.
	Length of tail	12 cm.

It must not be thought that the mammal population of Australia is composed entirely of marsupials and monotremes. These were probably the original inhabitants when, millions of years ago, Australia first became an island, but there have been many accidental introductions since then. A great many rodent species, perhaps floating ashore on driftwood, have survived and spread.

As an example, the Banana Rat (family *Muridae*) is found in many parts of Australia, as well as in New Guinea and the Solomon Islands. It is a fruit-eating arboreal (tree-living) rat, found in forests, and makes nests of grass in thick vegetation. Because the four new-born young cling to the mother's nipples, this animal was long thought to be a marsupial.

The word 'Bandicoot' comes from southern India, where it means 'pig rat', and was used inaccurately by early explorers to describe the nineteen species of Bandicoot now found in Australia, Tasmania, New Guinea and various islands. Differing habitats from plains to swamps are favoured by this family (*Peramelidae*). Some are carnivorous, others insectivorous or partially vegetarian.

The Short-nosed Bandicoot is widespread and common in many parts of Australia. Being nocturnal it is not often seen, but it is inoffensive—apart from its habit of digging holes in gardens. Two or three young, which develop quicker than those of any other marsupial, are born at a time, and there may be as many as three litters in a year.

Other species include the Long-nosed Bandicoot, the Rabbit-eared Bandicoot or Bilby, and the rare Pig-footed Bandicoot.

Cuscus (*Male above*)
(*Female below*)

| Length, head and body | 50 cm. |
| Length of tail | 45 cm. |

The marsupial family *Phalangeridae* contains about forty-two species. It includes the Cuscus, which resembles the Loris of Asia, the squirrel-like Possums, the mouse-like Phalangers and the Koala, which is like a small bear. This family has a wider range than most marsupials, being found in islands such as the Solomons and Timor, as well as in New Guinea, Tasmania and Australia itself.

All the *Phalangeridae* have beautiful woolly fur, and this has caused them to be persecuted to the point where many of them have had to be legally protected. They are mostly arboreal and nocturnal. In all, except the Koala, the pouch opens forward—as is the case with the Kangaroos. Different members of the family feed on leaves, fruit, buds, blossoms and their nectar, or insects.

The slow-moving Cuscus is found in New Guinea and some adjacent islands, and also in the northern (Cape York) part of Australia where it inhabits tropical forest. Cuscuses eat fruit and leaves, and also birds and their eggs.

Males and females are differently coloured, the males being spotted and the females generally of one colour. The young vary in colour and usually change as they mature. The tail is prehensile and is extensively used in climbing, and the big toe acts like a thumb when gripping a branch. The pouch is well developed and two young are born after a gestation period of only thirteen days.

Cuscuses emit a musky smell, but were nonetheless prized as food by the New Guineans—and also by their worst enemy, the python.

26

Brush-tailed Possum

Length, head and body 50 cm.
Length of tail 30 cm.

The Brush-tailed Possum (family *Phalangeridae*) is the largest and commonest of the Possums, and occupies a variety of habitats from forest and semi-desert to urban parks and gardens. Of all the Australian marsupials, it has best adapted itself to the coming of Man and will even occupy the lofts and roofs of his houses.

Because of its beautiful dense fur (known as 'Adelaide Chincilla'), the Brush-tailed Possum has been ruthlessly hunted—so much so that it has now to be protected. It occurs in most parts of Australia and Tasmania, and is one of the few marsupials to have been successfully introduced into New Zealand, where it has become a destructive pest. There is a great variety in coloration, golden, cream and black specimens being not uncommon in Tasmania.

A single young is born once a year after a gestation period of seventeen days. This compares with the fifty-eight days of the ordinary domestic cat, which is of similar body size. The young, which are pink and transparent, remain in the pouch for up to five months. When fully mature at about eighteen months, they have a curious brown area of fur on the chest, which is the site of a scent gland. This is used for establishing 'territorial rights' by rubbing against tree stumps. Many other mammals (for instance, deer, whose scent gland is situated below the eye) have similar organs.

This Possum is nocturnal and feeds principally on leaves and fruit, although birds are sometimes eaten. Apart from Man, its chief enemy is the Wedge-tailed Eagle.

Dormouse Possum *(above)*	Length, head and body	9 cm.
	Length of tail	8·5 cm.
Honey Possum *(below)*	Length, head and body	7·5 cm.
	Length of tail	9·5 cm.

The Possums (*Phalangeridae*) come in all sizes, the largest being cat-sized, and the smallest no bigger than a mouse. Because their habitats and modes of life are similar, they have come to resemble mammals elsewhere in the world which may be totally unrelated to them.

The Dormouse Possum provides a good example of this process. It is remarkably like the ordinary European Dormouse, not only in appearance but also in habits. It is nocturnal and arboreal, and becomes torpid or sluggish for as much as twelve days at a time in cold weather, making a nest of leaves and bark in a hollow log. In autumn, fat is stored in the base of the tail, which becomes greatly enlarged. Food consists of insects, spiders, fruit and the nectar from flowers.

Two litters a year of about five young are raised.

The hands of the Dormouse Possum are strikingly human in appearance, and the tail is partly prehensile. There are two species, one found in Tasmania and eastern Australia, and the other (shown here) in south-western Australia.

Also from south-western Australia comes the tiny Honey Possum with its long snout, specially adapted for probing into flowers for their nectar. Pollen and small insects are also eaten. For this diet they need few teeth, but have developed a very long tongue, tipped with bristles. The thin, wiry tail is almost hairless and fully prehensile.

Honey Possums build neat little nests, or will occupy deserted nests of birds. Four young are born at a time.

Ring-tailed Possum
(*above*)

Length, head and body	30 cm.
Length of tail	25 cm.

Lesser Gliding Possum, or 'Sugar Glider' (*below*)

Length, head and body	16 cm.
Length of tail	18 cm.

The word '*Phalangeridae*' means 'the fingered ones' and aptly describes the hands and feet of the Possums, Koalas and Cuscuses which make up this family. All have five digits on each limb; in some the first two fingers act like two 'thumbs', and on the foot the big toe acts like a thumb. In some of them, the second and third toes are joined together except at their tips.

One of the commonest Possums throughout Australia and Tasmania is the Ring-tailed, which occupies various habitats including built-up areas. There are about a dozen species of different sizes. These are arboreal animals with partially prehensile tails. Although they can sometimes be seen in daylight, sitting quite still in a tree, they are mostly nocturnal. They build large nests of leaves and ferns or, as with other possums, occupy a hollow tree. The diet is of leaves, fruit and flowers.

Only one litter a year is born, and this usually consists of two young.

Very different is the beautiful little 'Sugar Glider' which, like the flying squirrels, has skin membranes stretched between the limbs. On these it can glide for about fifty metres. Gliding Possums are found in New Guinea as well as on the eastern side of Australia and in Tasmania. They produce on average two young in each litter, and there are three species.

The 'Sugar Glider's' nest is built of leaves placed in a hollow tree, and in gathering them the animal hangs by its hind legs, collects the leaves with its fore feet and passes them back to the tail, which is then coiled round them and acts as a carrying device.

Koala

Length, head and body 60–80 cm.

The Koala is a strictly arboreal marsupial, found in eucalyptus forests in eastern Australia. Although sometimes incorrectly referred to as the 'Koala Bear', it is not in any way related to the bears and is a true member of the family *Phalangeridae*.

Koalas have hands specially adapted for climbing, in which the thumb and first finger oppose the remaining fingers when gripping a branch. They have a highly specialised digestive system which enables them to deal with a diet consisting almost exclusively of the leaves of certain kinds of eucalyptus. In consequence, the animal itself has a eucalyptus smell.

The word 'koala' is an Aboriginal word meaning 'no drink' but this is not strictly true. They have beautiful fur for which they have been terribly persecuted. Hundreds of thousands of koala skins were exported annually from Australia until protective laws were introduced. From near-extinction, the numbers have now increased, but Koalas are subject to various diseases, are vulnerable to many predators, and often fall victims to bush fires.

This attractive, rather slothful animal sleeps by day, but often without attempting to hide. One young a year is produced, which at birth is about the size of a bumble bee. At six months it leaves the backwards-facing pouch and, until it is a year old, is carried about on the mother's back.

Koalas usually live in small groups, often consisting of an adult male and several females with their young. Because of the problems of providing a correct diet, it is extremely difficult to keep them in captivity.

Common Wombat (Coarse-haired Wombat)

Length, head and body	100 cm.
Weight	35 kg.

There are several species of Wombat, placed in two genera, but both belonging to the marsupial family *Vombatidae*. They live in forests, grasslands or mountainous country in south-eastern Australia, Tasmania and on some islands in Bass Strait, and the much rarer Hairy-nosed Wombat occurs only on the Nullarbor Plain in south Australia, and possibly in parts of Queensland.

These rather bear-like animals are vegetarian and nocturnal, and make large burrows among tree roots or rocks. Some of these burrows are believed to have been in use for more than a hundred years and have assumed the proportions of caves. Wombats, though apparently clumsy, can move quite quickly, but they are inoffensive animals and many have been kept as pets and are said to be playful and affectionate.

Fossil remains indicate that there was once a Wombat species as big as a Hippopotamus. More than any other marsupial, they have features such as teeth and certain glands found among the rodents. The colour varies considerably from silver to black, and in the case of the Hairy-nosed Wombat at least, the fur has often been sought. The introduction into Australia of the rabbit, which competes with them for food, has probably contributed more than anything else to the decrease in their numbers.

Wombats, which are generally solitary animals, breed once a year, producing a single offspring. This is kept in a backward-facing pouch in the case of the Common Wombat, but in a forward-facing pouch for the rarer Hairy-nosed species.

Red Kangaroo

Length, head and body	140 cm.
Length of tail	100 cm.
Standing height	200 cm.

The Red Kangaroo and its related species, the Grey Kangaroo or 'Forester', are the largest marsupials. Together with the Wallaroo or Mountain Kangaroo, the Wallabies of various types, the Rat Kangaroos and the Tree Kangaroos, they are members of the marsupial family *Macropodidae*. This family contains fifty-five species, some of them extremely rare and many of them rapidly declining in numbers.

Red Kangaroos belong to the grass plains of inland Australia, while the Grey Kangaroo is found in scrub and woodland in eastern Australia and Tasmania. They are grazers and browsers, most active at night but are often seen sunning themselves in daylight, sometimes in quite large groups. They can exist for long periods without water, but will dig for it if necessary.

After a gestation period of thirty-three days, a single young measuring about 2 cm. is born, and climbs through the mother's fur to the large forward-facing pouch. At this time the mother weighs thirty thousand times the youngster's weight. Development is slow and the youngster (or 'joey') stays in the pouch for four months. It is weaned at one year and mature at two years old. Kangaroos continue to grow throughout their twenty-year life span, and elderly individuals can be enormous.

The Red Kangaroo, if cornered, delivers a savage kick from a heavily-clawed hind leg, but apart from Man it has few enemies, although the introduction of sheep and rabbits into its habitat has affected it adversely.

The female of this species tends to be greyer in colour, and is known as a 'blue flyer'.

Red-legged Scrub Wallaby (Pademelon) (above)	Length, head and body	70 cm.
	Length of tail	40 cm.
Northern Nail-tailed Wallaby (below)	Length, head and body	60 cm.
	Length of tail	50 cm.

Many species of Wallaby have seriously declined in numbers and range because of the introduction of predators and because of the competition afforded by domestic grazing animals.

Scrub Wallabies, one of four species, spread over Australia from Cape York in the north to Tasmania in the south. They are nocturnal forest animals, which prefer thick cover, and are both grazers and browsers. The tail is shorter than in other Wallabies, and they have the habit of thumping on the ground with their hind legs when alarmed. The Red-legged Scrub Wallaby (shown here) is also found in New Guinea. All four species produce single youngsters, and have been very extensively hunted for their skins.

The Nail-tailed Wallaby is one of three species, of which only the northern species, found in Northern Territory and Queensland, is at all numerous. The Bridled Nail-tailed and the Crescent-tailed of southern Australia are both distinguished by pale shoulder stripes, and are threatened with extinction. Like other marsupials brought into contact with Man, they have failed to adapt to the changed environment.

All three species produce a single youngster and have a curious nail on the tip of the tail, the function of which is unknown.

Nail-tailed Wallabies live in grass and scrub, and are sometimes referred to as 'organ grinders' due to their habit of carrying their arms outstretched and rotating them when hopping.

Pretty-faced Wallaby (Brush Wallaby) (*above*)

Length, head and body 45–105 cm.
Length of tail   33–75 cm.

Long-nosed Rat Kangaroo (Potoroo) (*below*)

Length, head and body   35 cm.
Length of tail   20 cm.

With only two exceptions, all members of the family *Macropodidae* progress by a series of hops or, when travelling fast, by considerable leaps. They are propelled only by the powerfully developed hind legs, the tail being used as a balance and as a prop when stationary. A large Kangaroo can jump as much as nine metres and travel at about 48 k.p.h. (30 m.p.h.) when necessary. Even the smallest members of the family are capable of surprising leaps and some of the quickest are the Brush Wallabies, of which there are eleven species.

These are found in brush and forest country through Australia, in Tasmania and in New Guinea and some adjacent islands. They are both grazers and browsers which have been much persecuted by cattle-men because of their competition to grazing stock. Many species, once numerous, are now becoming rare.

One young per litter is normal for these very attractively marked Wallabies, sometimes called 'whip-tails'.

Long-nosed Rat Kangaroos, or Potoroos, are still common in Tasmania, but are now rare in southern Australia. Of the three species, two are now virtually extinct. Forest and scrub are favoured habitats and, like other members of the *Macropodidae*, Potoroos are mainly nocturnal. Plants and their roots, for which the Potoroo digs characteristic holes, form the diet.

The hind legs are relatively short, but the structure of the toes is the same as with other *Macropods*—the first toe missing, the second and third toes small and joined by skin, a huge fourth toe and a smaller fifth toe.

Ring-tailed Rock	Length, head and body	70 cm.
Wallaby (*above*)	Length of tail	60 cm.
Hare Wallaby (*below*)	Length, head and body	40 cm.
	Length of tail	35 cm.

Broadly speaking, the Kangaroos and Wallabies are the mammal equivalent, in Australia, of the antelope and deer in other continents, and like them, they occupy varying habitats and range in size from giants to pygmies. To a certain extent also, the smallest members of the *Macropodidae*, such as the Rat Kangaroos and Hare Wallabies, are the equivalent of the hares and rabbits elsewhere.

The Ring-tailed Rock Wallaby, with its curious coloration, is found among rocky outcrops principally in southern Australia, although a few still remain in Queensland and in western New South Wales. There are about six species. They set up 'camps' in a suitable area and occupy it for many years—the passage of their padded feet imparting quite a glossy surface to the rock face. They are most agile climbers, and eat grass and the bark of young trees. The litter consists of one youngster. They are now becoming rare.

Rare, too, are the Hare Wallabies, of which there are three species occupying separate areas from Queensland to south-western Australia, and on several small islands. Some of them look remarkably like hares and behave in much the same way, including a sort of 'dance'. When chased they whistle and are capable of great speed and enormous leaps.

They have always been hunted for food by the aborigines, and now, under added pressure from farming and predators, they have been much reduced in numbers and range. Not much is known about their breeding habits, but they are believed to make nests somewhat similar to the 'form' of a hare.

Tree Kangaroo

Length, head and body	*65 cm.*
Length of tail	*75 cm.*

Two species of Tree Kangaroo (family *Macropodidae*) inhabit the tropical forest of north-eastern Queensland. These are Lumholtz's Kangaroo (seen here) and Bennet's Tree Kangaroo. Three other species are found throughout New Guinea, from whence it is believed the Tree Kangaroos reached Australia. Many of these species have dense, brightly-coloured fur, and all of them are fully arboreal.

Tree Kangaroos inhabit very remote areas, and little is known about them, but they are believed to live in small groups and to produce one young per litter. They feed on leaves and fruit.

Tree Kangaroos have evolved from the Wallabies, and are now equipped with wide paws with rough pads and curved claws. The tail is not prehensile, but is very extensively used as a counter-balance and prop in climbing. In particular, the tail seems to act as a rudder when this unusual marsupial leaps from branch to branch, or from tree to ground, which can be as far as eighteen metres.

The fur on the nape of the neck and on parts of the back grows from back to front; it is believed to assist in shedding rain. Movement on the ground is a series of hops, somewhat awkward in manner as the hind legs are not greatly developed, and the fore limbs are of almost the same length. On the ground the tail is held rigidly upwards.

Tree Kangaroos are not rare and have escaped the persecution and changes in their habitat to which so many marsupials have been subjected.

Dingo

Length, head and body   90 cm.
Length of tail   35 cm.

Between twenty-five and thirty thousand years ago, aboriginal man reached Australia, which for millions of years had remained cut off from the rest of the world. With him in his boats he brought a semi-domesticated dog—the Dingo. This animal, a true carnivore of the family *Canidae*, ran wild throughout the continent and, because it was more intelligent, almost exterminated animals such as the Thylacine (p. 20) which had previously been the dominant ground-dwelling predator.

The Dingo never reached Tasmania, where the ousted predators are now found.

When Europeans arrived in Australia about two hundred years ago, they introduced cattle and sheep and the Dingo started to prey on them. So, in its turn, it has now been very largely exterminated in parts of Australia, but it would be a pity if this animal, possibly representing one of the original ancestors of our domestic dogs, were to disappear altogether.

Man has made the mistake of introducing many other species into Australia's marsupial world. The rabbit has cost millions of pounds in damage; the fox, the cat and some others have destroyed much of the native fauna. However, the greatest damage has been done by the introduction of sheep which, although to Man's benefit, has done tremendous harm in destroying the habitat and grazing areas of the native animals. Kangaroos and Wallabies have been driven from the grassland, and great areas of brush and forest, with their inhabitants, cleared for new farmland. As a result Australia's mammals have suffered tremendous and irreparable losses.

Species introduced into New Zealand
(*not shown to scale*)

Apart from two species of Bat and one Rat, New Zealand has no native mammals at all. However, it does have a bird population of great interest, beauty and variety.

During his second voyage to New Zealand in 1774, Captain Cook introduced the European Wild Pig as a source of food. Since then, and particularly during the nineteenth century, Man has introduced many species, nearly all of which have proved disastrous to the wild life of New Zealand, and have become pests.

The Rabbit came, as a food source, in 1838, and in 1858 the Brush-tailed Possum in an attempt to start a fur industry. Stoats and Weasels, introduced in 1885 to control the Rabbits, did nothing more than destroy many birds. In 1881, the Red Deer was introduced for sport and has since become a serious menace. The Wild Goat, the Chamois, the Himalayan Tahr, the Sambar and even the Moose were brought in for the same purpose; most of them still survive, but not in great numbers.

Rats and Mice must have arrived early (and uninvited) in ships; Hedgehogs and Hares, and other species from Europe have established themselves, but curiously enough, repeated attempts to introduce Wallabies have met with only partial success.

Sheep farming has seriously altered the New Zealand landscape, and the introduced mammals, wild and domestic, have greatly reduced the unique population of birds and their habitat. Some species are approaching extinction and others have already vanished.

RED DEER
(SCOTLAND)

STOAT
(ENGLAND)

TAHR
(INDIA)

WILD PIG
(EUROPE)

BRUSH-TAILED
POSSUM
(AUSTRALIA)

CHAMOIS
(AUSTRIA)

WILD GOAT
(EUROPE)

HARE
(ENGLAND)

INDEX